HEUNI

Helsinki Institute for Crime Prevention and Control, affiliated with the United Nations

Criminal Justice Systems in Europe

ENGLAND AND WALES

Gordon C. Barclay

**Helsinki
Finland
1990**

Valtion painatuskeskus
Kampin VALTIMO
Helsinki 1990

TABLE OF CONTENTS

LIST OF ILLUSTRATIONS

1. INTRODUCTION

1.1   Historical differences in how the legal system has developed within the individual countries which make up the United Kingdom have meant that England and Wales (together), Scotland and Northern Ireland should be looked at separately.   The current paper only attempts to cover England and Wales, briefly setting out the criminal justice system as it now operates.

1.2   In 1988, 50 million out of a total United Kingdom population of 57 million lived in England and Wales.   About three-quarters of the population live in urban areas which make up 14 per cent of the total land area.   Currently, 4.5 per cent of the population of Great Britain (England, Wales and Scotland) are from ethnic minority groups.   About two-thirds are of West Indian/Guyanese, Indian or Pakistani ethnic origin.   The majority of recent immigration from the Commonwealth to this country has been to the major conurbations in England.   In 1988, 8 per cent of the working population in England and Wales were unemployed, although unemployment was lower in the south-east of England which includes the London area.

2. HISTORICAL DEVELOPMENT OF CRIMINAL LAW AND PROCEDURES.

2.1   The present legal system in England and Wales traces its origins back to the twelfth century, and the rapid expansion of institutions which followed the conquest of England by Duke William of Normandy in 1066. Before that time, there were differences of detail, particularly of procedure in each of the thirty-two counties into which England was divided.   Unlike the rest of Europe, where countries based themselves on Roman law, the system of English common law, as it was called, developed uniquely.   This system was based upon two principal courts, the Commons Bench and the Kings Bench.   Around 1200 saw the appearance of a class of professional attorneys who were allowed to represent their clients in litigation. The system however, was centralised and this had to be reconciled with the need for local investigation and trial. There developed therefore, the major court of common law (the "assizes") and it was not until 1972[1] with the introduction of the Crown Court, that these institutions were finally abolished.

2.2   Within Wales, a separate legal system had grown up and even after the invasion of Wales by Edward I of England in 1304, no attempt was made to substitute English for Welsh law. It was not until 1535 that Wales was finally incorporated into the common law framework. In Scotland, a system based upon Roman law developed. Following the merger of the Parliaments of Scotland and England and Wales in 1707, no attempt was made to unite the two systems and so both systems develop today side by side.

2.3   The law in England and Wales may be divided into two, viz:
a) **The Common Law**, which is made up of those general customs which have been regarded as laws in the land from time immemorial. By general agreement endorsed by the practice of courts, certain rules of conduct have by custom become laws, and offences under these laws are termed common law offences - (for example, affray and conspiracy). A substantial proportion of Common Law is termed Case Law, built up from historical precedence.

b) **The Statute Law**, which includes all the laws made by direct order of the State and set out in Acts of Parliament or statutes. Many offences which were originally common law offences have been dealt with by an Act of Parliament; hence an offence may be both a common law and statutory offence.

2.4   There is currently no Criminal Code for England and Wales. Recently, the Law Commission published a proposal for a Criminal Code[2] with a draft Criminal Code Bill. This report identified over 7,000 offences but thought that there were probably more since it was now impossible to identify all existing offences. Recent discussions on this Code[3] have highlighted the difficulties of finding sufficient time in the already busy Parliamentary timetable to introduce a bill to set up such a code and of ensuring that it could be regularly amended. There is therefore no present timetable for introducing a criminal code.

2.5   The other agencies of the criminal justice system are much later in origin than courts or the legal profession. The Police and Prison Service were set up nationally in the last century, the probation service at the beginning of this century and the Crown Prosecution Service as recently as 1986. Their present organisation are covered in detail later in this paper.

3. ORGANISATION OF CRIMINAL JUSTICE

GOVERNMENT

3.1   There is no Ministry of Justice covering criminal justice within England and Wales.   Three Government Departments share this responsibility, viz.

a) **The Home Office**, which deals with matters relating to the police, prisons, probation and the magistrates' courts.   It is the main department dealing with changes in the criminal law and in sentencing practice.   The Home Secretary has also general responsibility for internal security.

b)   **The Lord Chancellor's Department**, which deals with matters relating to the judiciary, administers Higher Courts (including the Crown Court) and is responsible for Legal Aid. The Lord Chancellor is, as well as being the leading legal figure in the country, a member of the Cabinet and the Speaker of the House of Lords.

c)   **The Crown Prosecution Service**, which is responsible for the independent prosecution of nearly all criminal offences instituted by the police.   It is headed by the Director of Public Prosecutions and is under the superintendence of the Attorney General.

POLICE

3.2   There are about 125,000 police officers in England and Wales who have, since local government was reorganised in 1974, been divided into 43 police forces. 41 forces (excluding the London area) are headed by Chief Constables who report to a local police authority or police committee[4] made up of locally elected representatives (including local magistrates). In the Metropolitan Police (covering London), the Commissioner of Police of the Metropolis, because of his wider powers for security, reports directly to the Home Secretary. Finally, the Commissioner of City of London Police reports to "The Common Council" of the City of London.

3.3   Within the police forces, there are about 47,000 civilians, which includes Traffic Wardens, who handle parking offences. An Inspectorate under Her Majesty's Chief Inspector of Constabulary within the Home Office provides a central inspectorate role on police forces. In addition, a number of special law enforcement agencies have been established to combat specific types of crime, eg. Regional Crime Squads (9); Serious Fraud Squad; National Drugs Intelligence Unit and National Football Intelligence Unit. Matters relating to offences committed on trains are handled by the British Transport Police and a separate force handles Ministry of Defence establishments.

COURTS

3.4   In 1972 following the Courts Act[1] the courts of assize and quarter sessions were replaced by a single **Crown Court** with power to sit anywhere in England and Wales. It is part of the Supreme Court. The Court has jurisdiction to deal with all trials on indictment and with persons committed for sentence, and to hear appeals from lower Courts, including juvenile cases. The Act imposed no geographical limitations on the catchment area Crown Court centres, with County and district boundaries having no statutory significance in determining where a case should be heard. In practice most Crown Court cases are heard at the centre most convenient to the magistrates' court which committed the case for trial. The more serious offences can be tried only by a High Court, judge, others may be dealt with by any circuit, judge or recorder. There are currently about 90 courts of the Crown Court divided into 6 regions, known as Circuits.

3.5   Offences may be dealt with summarily at a **magistrates' court**. This is defined[5] as a court of summary jurisdiction or justices and includes a single examining justice. Such a court acts in a petty sessional court-house for a petty sessions area, although further court-houses may be set up. The case may be tried either by at least two justices ("lay magistrates") or by a stipendiary (legally qualified) magistrate who sits alone[6]. Justices are appointed for life by the Crown (retiring at the age of 70) and receive no salary (only expenses). They have no legal training, in general, before appointment, and usually have full-time jobs in most walks of life. Magistrates' courts other than juvenile courts are normally open to the public. Justices are normally restricted to ordering sentences of imprisonment of not more than 6 months or fines exceeding £2,000. For offences triable-either-way (see Para 4.3) if more severe sentences are thought necessary, the offender may be committed to the Crown Court for sentence. Magistrates' courts in England and Wales are divided into just under 550 petty sessional divisions, each independent and under 105 local Magistrates' Courts Committee. A recent report[7] has advocated the setting up of an administrative structure for the courts, possibly considering them as a separate agency. Currently, further consideration is being given to these proposals.

3.6   Within the magistrates' courts, certain are designated as **Juvenile Courts**. Such a court is composed of specially trained justices and deals only with charges against and applications relating to children and young persons. It should in most circumstances only deal with persons under 17 who are not jointly charged with adults[8]. It sits apart from other courts and is not open to the public. It consists of not more than three justices, including one man, and one woman or one stipendiary magistrate. A recent Home Office White Paper[9] has suggested the renaming of this court as the **Youth Court** and including also persons aged 17.

3.7   The Higher Courts include the Supreme Court which consists of a) **the Court of Appeal**; b) **the High Court** and c) **the Crown Court**. A person convicted at a magistrates' court may appeal to the Crown Court, while a person convicted at the Crown Court may appeal to the Court of Appeal and finally to the House of Lords. Appeals on points of law and proceedings arising in the magistrates' courts are dealt with by the Queen's Bench, Divisional Court of the High Court. It has very limited jurisdiction in such matters arising in the Crown Court. The highest court in the land is The High Court of Parliament or the **House of Lords**. This court is composed of the Lords of Appeal, who are lawyers of eminence generally appointed from amongst the judges of the Court of Appeal. On appointment they are made life peers and are thus members of the House of Lords. They deal with points of law of general public importance brought before them on appeal from the **Supreme Court**.

PROBATION SERVICE

3.8   Since the 1974 reorganisation of local authorities, the probation service has been divided up into 56 areas. In each area, there is a probation and after-care committee. The majority of those on these committees are justices drawn from the local courts, but persons are co-opted from other fields as well.

3.9   There are about 6,750 probation officers who supervise the orders imposed on offenders including probation, community service, suspended sentence supervision and money payment supervision. Offenders imprisoned will also receive pre- and post-release after-care, both statutory and voluntary. A small proportion of the caseload of probation officers (about 5 per cent) is domestic supervision including matrimonial and wardship supervision.

3.10   A probation inspectorate within the Home Office supervises the work of the service. Discussion papers issued by the Home Office in 1990 on the probation service included the proposal that the service should be nationally organised [10] and that there was a role for the voluntary and private sectors in the supervision of offenders[11].

PRISON SERVICE

3.11   Within the Home Office, the Prison Service accommodates a current prison population of 46,650. The service is currently organised in 4 regions under a Director-General who chairs the non-statutory Prison

Board[12]. Establishments are divided into those dealing with female prisoners, sentenced adult prisoners, sentenced young offenders (under 21 years of age) and adult prisoners and young offenders on remand. The young offender institutions replaced detention centres and youth custody centres for young offenders on 1 October 1988. The Rules governing prison establishments were initially laid under the Prison Act[13] in 1964[14] for adult prisoners and the Young Offender Institution Statutory instrument in 1988[15] for young offenders.

3.12   The current organisation in prison establishments was built around the "fresh start" proposals, introduced in 1987-88, that were designed to introduce a more flexible approach to the work of the prison service. This approach substantially reduced the hours worked by prison officers and has been accompanied by a substantial recruitment programme. Further re-organisation is now in progress including the relocation of headquarters from London and the abolition of the current regional structure.

CROWN PROSECUTION SERVICE

3.13   Up until 1985, the main prosecuting authority was the police. The Crown Prosecution Service[16] (CPS) was introduced initially in Metropolitan areas and then throughout England and Wales as an independent national body.   However, a number of forces had, in anticipation of the creation of the CPS, begun to re-organise their prosecution arrangements, creating central administrative or operational support units with responsibility for preparing cases for prosecution. The CPS has over 100 local offices which are responsible for the conduct of all police-initiated prosecutions (save for certain minor traffic offences to which a defendant pleads guilty).   The CPS is organised into 31 areas covering England and Wales, usually aligned with one, or sometimes two, police force areas.   Areas are sub-divided into 2 or more Branches, headed by a Chief Crown Prosecutor.   There also exists a relatively small Headquarters based in London.   The CPS, after considering the papers supplied by the police, has the right to discontinue the proceedings if it is felt that the evidence was insufficient or that this is in the public interest.

4. PROCEDURES WITHIN THE CRIMINAL JUSTICE SYSTEM

DETECTION AND CHARGING

4.1   Following the detection of an alleged offender for a crime, the options open to the police are:

No further action - the police may decide to take no action because they consider there is insufficient evidence to prosecute or that an informal warning may be sufficient. This will include cases where the suspects are children under ten years who are below the age of criminal responsibility[17]. Such children may be dealt with under the civil law. Children between the ages of ten and fourteen years cannot be considered for an offence unless it can be proved that they knew that they were doing wrong.

Cautioning - Where an offender admits his or her guilt, a formal caution may be given by a senior police officer. Although frequently used for juveniles and first time offenders, it is increasingly been used for older offenders and subsequent offences. No further action is needed by the offender.

Charging - When an accused person is charged, information is laid before a justice to the effect that some person is suspected of having committed an offence[18]. This will result in either a **warrant to arrest** or a **summons**. Warrants may only be issued where a) the offence is indictable (see below) or is punishable with imprisonment or b) the address of the accused is not sufficiently established for a summons to be served. No branch of the executive or the judiciary can direct a police officer to bring a prosecution (or not to do so) in a particular case - this will include Ministers of the Crown[19].

REMANDS

4.2   A defendant may either be bailed by the court on recognizance with, or without, sureties to appear before a court or by the police without recognizance. Alternatively, a defendant will be remanded in custody and the case is adjourned, whilst papers are prepared for the trial. A magistrates' court has the power to remand any person in custody for up to 8 days, experiments are currently being carried out in 4 courts to increase this period to 28 days. The grounds for refusing bail were set out in the 1976 Bail Act[20] and are that the defendant would -

    a)   fail to surrender to custody, or

    b)   commit an offence while on bail, or

    c)   interfere with witnesses, or otherwise obstruct the course of justice, whether in relation to himself or any other person.

4.3   In addition to the general grounds for refusing bail, a juvenile under 17 may be refused bail if the court is satisfied that he should be kept in custody for his own protection. Juveniles refused bail must be remanded to the care of the local authority. There is an exception in the case of 15 or 16 year old boys. They may be remanded in Prison Department custody if they are certified by the courts as being too unruly to be safely committed to the care of the local authority.

CATEGORIES OF OFFENCES

4.4   Three separate types of offences were defined under the 1977 Criminal Law Act[21]. Offences are either:

    a) Triable only on indictment, which are the most serious breaches of the criminal law and are triable by a judge and jury at the Crown Court. These "indictable only" offences include murder, manslaughter, rape and robbery.

    b) Triable-either-way, which may either be tried at the Crown Court or a magistrates' court.

    c) Summary, which are triable only at a magistrates' court. This group is dominated by motoring offences.

Criminal damage may be tried summarily if the value of property involved does not exceed £2,000 (£400 up to October 1988); otherwise it is triable-either-way.

PROCEEDINGS AT MAGISTRATES' COURT

4.5   About 2,000,000 defendants are prosecuted annually in magistrates' courts; 460,000 for indictable offences (including triable-either-way), 600,000 for summary non-motoring offences and 900,000 for summary motoring offences.   If the Crown Prosecution Service feel there is insufficient evidence such that there is not a realistic prospect of conviction it may exercise its power under section 23 of the Prosecution of Offences Act 1985 to discontinue the proceedings either before or after the hearing.   It may alternatively consider that the available evidence supports a different charge.   The Crown Prosecution Service discontinued about 130,000 cases in 1989.

4.6   About one in five indictable offences (including triable-either-way) are committed annually to the Crown Court.   The reasons for **committing** offences to the Crown Court are either:

     a)   where the offence is triable only on indictment and the magistrates' hearing only a preliminary one;

     b)   where the offence is triable-either-way and the defendant is committed for trial on indictment.   This committal results either from a direction by the magistrate or an election for trial by the defendant.

     c)   where the offence is triable-either-way and the defendant is tried summarily, but the court felt that a sentence should be given above its limits (ie: over 6 months imprisonment or £2,000 fine).   The defendant is **committed** to the Crown Court **for sentence**.

4.7   Where an offence may be tried only on indictment and an accused person is legally represented, a magistrates' court may, with his agreement, commit him to the Crown Court for trial without any consideration of the evidence.   In all other cases, the magistrates' court must examine the strength of the evidence and decide whether it warrants committal for trial. If not, the defendant has to be discharged.

4.8   For a triable-either-way offence, magistrates have to follow a set procedure in considering whether to try the case themselves or to commit to the Crown Court for trial. Firstly, the prosecution and defence have to be invited to indicate whether in their view the case is one which may suitably be dealt with summarily. If after hearing both sides the magistrates feel the case is too serious for them to deal with within theirs powers, they proceed to commit to the Crown Court. If the magistrates feel the case may be tried summarily, the defendant may still exercise his right to be tried by jury and the case can be committed for trial. Just over one half of cases are committed at the magistrates' request. In making their decisions, magistrates have no knowledge of the defendant's circumstances and any previous convictions.

4.9   Frequently, an accused person will be charged with several offences, some of them triable-either way and some summary. If the triable-either-way offences are committed for trial, certain summary offences [22] may also be included on the indictment, ie: driving while disqualified, common assault and taking a motor vehicle without authority, but the Crown Court may only deal with them in the manner in which a magistrates' court could have dealt with them. Other offences must be dealt with summarily.

PROCEEDINGS BEFORE MAGISTRATES

4.10   On summary trial the court, if the accused appears, will tell him the charge and ask him whether he pleads guilty or not. After hearing the evidence from the parties, the court shall convict the accused or dismiss the case. If the accused pleads guilty, the court may convict him without hearing evidence. If the prosecutor appears but the accused fails to appear as requested, the court on proof of service of summons may proceed in his absence or adjourn the hearing. If the accused appears but the prosecutor does not, the court may dismiss the case or adjourn the trial. A court in which a person was convicted, in addition to dealing with them in any other way, may make a "compensation order" requiring the offender to pay compensation to the victim for any personal injury, loss or damage resulting from that offence.

TRIAL BY JURY

4.11   A jury consists of 12 persons called at random from the list of all those persons aged 18 to 70 who registered as electors. These jurors take an oath to well and truly try the case and to give a true verdict according to the evidence.   The duty of the jury is to listen to the evidence and to give their verdict whether the prisoner is innocent or guilty. The accused has the right to challenge any juror for cause but he may no longer challenge without cause.[23]   The verdict of the jury in criminal proceedings need not be unanimous. If guilty, the judge of the court pronounces sentence. If convicted, the offender may appeal to the Court of Appeal and may have a further appeal to the House of Lords. As at the magistrates' court a "compensation" order may be awarded to the victim and such orders at both courts have recently been encouraged[24]. The court may order the accused if convicted to pay the whole or any part of the costs incurred to be paid by the accused to the prosecution.   The court may also, on acquittal, order the payment of defence costs by the prosecutor.

PROCEEDINGS INVOLVING JUVENILES

4.12   Young people aged between 10 and 16 inclusive, are tried in the juvenile court comprising specially trained magistrates.   No person is allowed to be present, unless authorised by the court, except for the members and officers of the court, parties to the case, their legal representatives, witnesses and bona fide representatives of the media. Proceedings may be reported in the press but the juveniles may not be identified. A juvenile is tried in the juvenile court regardless of his alleged offence unless he is:

  a)   charged with homicide (ie: murder or manslaughter) when he must be committed to the Crown Court for trial.

b) aged 14 or more and charged with an offence for which an adult could be imprisoned for at least 14 years. If the juvenile court considers that a longer custodial sentence than the juvenile court has power to impose should be available if the juvenile is convicted, he may be committed to the Crown Court for trial.

c) charged jointly with another aged 17 or more when both may be dealt with in an adult court.

SENTENCING

4.13   In sentencing an offender, the judge or magistrate will take account of:

a) **The facts of the offence**, which have been presented in court. In addition, a defendant pleading guilty may wish to admit other similar offences and the courts have adopted the practice of **taking offences into consideration** without the offender being formally convicted of them.

b)   **The circumstances of the offender**.   The prosecution will provide a statement known as "the antecedents" covering domestic circumstances, previous convictions and sentences. In addition, for serious offences, a **social inquiry report** giving fuller information will usually be prepared for the court by a probation officer. This report contains information about the character, personality and social and domestic background of the defendant; educational record and information about employment (if any). This report may include comments on possible sentences.

c) **Plea in mitigation**. In more serious cases an offender will be represented either by a barrister (counsel) or by a solicitor. The defence lawyer will make a speech in mitigation on behalf of the offender to give the court the defendant's explanation of the offence and any other matters going in the defendant's favour.

a probation officer or the local authority (in the person of a local authority social worker). A wide range of requirements may be attached to the order relating to accommodation and activities.

i) Discharge

4.28   A court may discharge a person either absolutely or conditionally where the court takes the view that it is not necessary to inflict punishment. For an absolute discharge, no further action is required. However, in a conditional discharge (the majority of discharges), the offender remains liable to punishment for the offence if he is convicted of a further offence within whatever period (not more than three years) that the court may specify.

j) Further sentences

4.29   A range of other further punishment are used but to a lesser extent. These include binding over (either to keep the peace or be of good behaviour), attendance centre orders and care orders. Under attendance centre orders, offenders under 21 may be ordered to take part in a structured programme of activities on Saturday afternoons for a set number of weeks. Care orders are available for convicted offenders under 17 and place the young people in the care of the Local authority. (Courts' power to make care orders in criminal proceedings will be abolished when the Childrens Act 1989 comes into force). Trials have recently taken place into the use of electronic monitoring as an alternative to remand in custody. The recent White Paper [9] suggested a new sentence of a curfew order enforced using electronic monitoring.

PAROLE AND REMISSION

4.30   Remission of sentence, under the Prison Rules, is available to anyone serving a sentence of imprisonment of more than five days. Remission will be granted automatically unless forfeited (wholly or in part) for an offence against prison discipline. Parole is, on the other hand, a discretionary and conditional system of release. It applies only to determinate sentenced prisoners who have:

- served at least one-third of the sentence imposed by the court.
- served at least six months in prison, excluding any time on remand.
- been recommended for release by the Parole Board (or the Local Review Committee at the prison) and approved for release by the Home Secretary.

4.31   Since 1987[29] remission was increased from one-third to one-half of sentence of 12 months or less; for longer sentences it remains one-third of the term imposed by the court. In addition, the Home Secretary announced on 30 November 1983 that prisoners sentenced to more than 5 years for offences of violence, sex, arson and drug trafficking offences, were to be granted parole under supervision for at most a few months before the end of sentence other than in exceptional circumstances. New arrangements are envisaged in the recent White Paper,[9] which would make the time actually served in prison closer to the sentence originally ordered by the court. The present system of remission and parole would be replaced. All prisoners would serve at least one-half of their sentences in custody. For those sentenced to less than four years, release would take place automatically after 50 per cent of sentence, subject to good behaviour in prison. For those service sentences of four years or more, discretionary parole would be available after 50 per cent of sentence has been served and, if not granted, release would take place after two-thirds of sentence. All young offenders and all adults serving more than 12 months would be subject to Statutory Supervision on release until 75 per cent of sentence. Any prisoner committing an offence between release and the 100 per cent point of sentence would be liable to recall to prison to serve the balance of the original sentence outstanding at the time the fresh offence was committed.

5. THE POSITION OF THE VICTIM

5.1   There is a generous Criminal Injuries Compensation Scheme for those injured as a result of crime, whatever their nationality. Compensation covers pain and suffering and loss of facility as well as loss of earnings and future loss of earnings.

5.2   Local victim support schemes, funded by the Home Office, through a national office, cover 94 per cent of the population of England and Wales and provide help and guidance to individual victims of crime. A recent Government paper[30] has been issued setting out the rights of victims and how they should be treated by the various criminal justice services.

5.3   Where the Crown Prosecution Service declines to prosecute, victims are entitled to prosecute privately, but seldom do. Following conviction, the courts can award compensation on its own or combined with other penalties. Such orders are awarded in about 13 per cent of cases in magistrates' courts and 9 per cent in the Crown Court. Recent Legislation[31] requires the court to give reasons for not making a compensation order when it could have been done.

6. RECENT GOVERNMENT PUBLICATIONS

6.1   In 1990 a series of Government papers have been issued dealing with Criminal Justice matters. These are:

"Crime, Justice and Protecting the Public", (HMSO, 1990) - which sets out the Government's proposals for a new statutory framework for sentencing and changes to the Parole system.

"Supervision and Punishment in the Community: "A framework for action" (HMSO, 1990) - A discussion paper which canvasses options for change to the organisation of the probation service.

"Victim's Charter: A Statement of the Rights of Victims of Crime" (HMSO, 1990).

"Partnership in dealing with offenders in the Community" (HMSO, 1990) - A discussion paper on the greater involvement of the voluntary section in dealing with offenders.

7. CURRENT STATISTICAL TRENDS (Table 1)

A. OFFENCES RECORDED BY THE POLICE (Figure 1)

7.1   The main measure used of the amount of crime with which the police are faced, is statistics on notifiable offences recorded. However, offences may either not be reported to the police or not recorded by them. From the 1988 British Crime Survey[32] based upon interviews with households, estimates suggest that the increases in actual crime have been lower than recorded by the police.

7.2   In 1989, the police recorded 3.9 million notifiable offences of which 93 per cent were against property, 6 per cent against the person and the remaining 1 per cent were other types of crime. The total number of crimes recorded in 1989 was 4 per cent higher than in 1988. This increase follows a 5 per cent fall in 1988 and compares with a 5 per cent annual average increase between 1980 and 1987.

7.3   Offences of theft account for just over one half of recorded notifiable offences, and the most frequent types of theft are of, or from, motor vehicles, which account for over a quarter of all offences. Offences of burglary, mainly involving property of small value, account for a further fifth.

Table 1   **The operation of criminal justice system in England and Wales, 1979-1989 : key indicators**

	1979	1986	1989
Notifiable offences recorded by the police (thousands)	2,537	3,849	3,870
- cleared up %	41	32	34
Persons found guilty or cautioned[1] (thousands)			
- aged 10-16	164	142	119[2]
- aged 17-20	111	126	128[2]
- aged 21 and over	234	252	277[2]
Use of fines[1]	50	39	39[2]
Use of custody[1]			
- aged 14-16 (%)	10.9	10.6	10.1[2]
- aged 17-20 (%)	16.6	19.0	18.2[2]
- aged 21 and over (%)	17.3	19.2	18.4[2]
Average prison population (thousands)			
- Unsentenced	6.1	10.1	10.5
- Sentenced	35.6	36.6	37.9
- Non criminal	0.5	0.2	0.2
Average sentence length[3] (months)	18.6	18.1	19.0[2]

(1)   Indictable offences only
(2)   1988 figures as 1989 not yet available
(3)   Adult males at the Crown Court

Figure 1

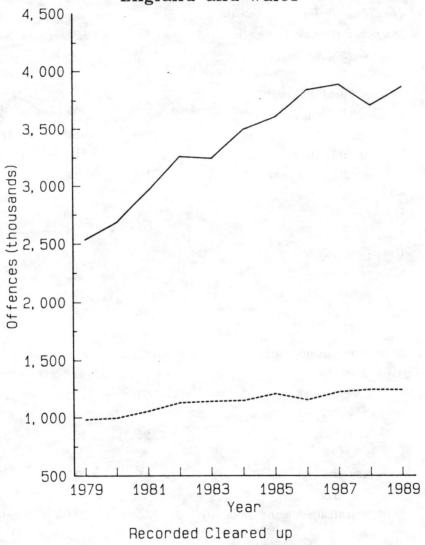

Notifiable offences recorded by the police
England and Wales

7.4   There were 240,000 violent crimes recorded in 1989, of which 74 per cent were violence against the person, 14 per cent were robberies and 12 per cent sexual offences.   Offences of violence against the person increased by 12 per cent in 1989, as in 1987 and 1988, compared with an average increase of 4 per cent a year between 1980 and 1986.   However, over 90 per cent of such offences were minor woundings.   Sexual offences also rose by 12 per cent in 1989.   Most of this increase was accounted for by indecent assaults on females, which form the biggest single category; recorded rapes rose by 16 per cent in 1989, as in 1988.   The increases in rapes are thought to result from a higher proportion of allegations of rape being recorded as crimes.

7.5   In 1989, 34 per cent of all offences were cleared up by the police; 30 per cent for property offences and 70 per cent for offences involving violence.   For offences cleared up 51 per cent resulted in an offender being charged or summonsed for an offence, 11 per cent in caution, 17 per cent were offences taken into consideration and the remaining 21 per cent includes admissions by prisoners of previous offences where no charge is made.

B.   OFFENDERS

7.6   The peak age for known offending was 15-18 years for males and 15 years for females in 1988 (the latest year for which figures are available).   This is based upon the number of offenders either convicted by the courts or cautioned by the police, relative to population.   About 45 per cent of all known offenders were aged under 21.   Currently about 72 per cent of juvenile offenders (aged 10-16) are cautioned, 18 per cent of those aged 17-20 and 16 per cent of those aged over 21.   Recent initiatives, including the setting up of local Juvenile Liaison Panels in many areas, have increased the use of cautioning for juveniles and also resulted in the use of other less formal methods of dealing with juveniles outside the main criminal justice system.   It is hoped that current Government initiatives will extend cautioning into the older age groups.

C. SENTENCING

7.7   **Fines** - The fine is the most frequently used disposal, with 90 per cent of offenders sentenced for summary non-motoring offences and 97 per cent of those sentenced for summary motoring offences are fined. For indictable offences (including triable-either-way) the fine is still the most frequent disposal but accounts for only 40 per cent of sentences. Since the early 1970's, the use of the fine has fallen substantially for indictable offences and it has only been in the last year that it has begun to rise again.

7.8   **Custody** - Following a long period in which the annual numbers sentenced to custody increased, in the last year (1989), both the numbers sentenced and the use of custody have fallen at both magistrates' courts and the Crown Court. At the magistrates' courts, the fall in the use of custody for indictable offences has been from 8 per cent in 1986 to just over 5 per cent in 1989, while at the Crown Court, the fall has been from 52 to 46 per cent. A small part (1-2 percentage points) of this fall reflects the re-classification in October 1989 of certain offences (eg: driving while disqualified) from being an indictable offence to a summary offence. Such recent falls have been most significant for young adults where the number sentenced annually to custody for indictable offences have fallen in one year by about one-third to 14,000.

7.9   Over the last few years, there has been a gradual increase in the sentence lengths awarded for the most violent offenders, including a rise for rape offences from 4 years in 1984 to 6 years in 1988. Further recent increases have also occurred resulting from the use of non-custodial disposals for the less serious offences. For adults at magistrates' courts, the average sentence length was about 3 months while at the Crown Court the overall average was 19 months. For burglary the average was 17 months, robbery 48 months, violence against the person 19 months, and drugs offences 27 months.

7.10   **Non-custodial** - For those sentenced for indictable offences, about 11 per cent are sentenced to a probation order, and 7 per cent to a community service order and 15 per cent are given a discharge. The recent drop in the numbers sentenced to custody has resulted in a greater use of probation/community service orders at the Crown Court, while at magistrates' courts the main increase has been in discharges suggesting a general movement down-tariff.

D. PRISON POPULATION (Figure 2)

7.11   The prison population has risen over the last decade to reach an average of 49,900 in 1988. However, recent drops in the use of custody have meant that the population fell in 1989 to an average of 48,600. This population is made up of sentenced prisoners (37,900), untried or unsentenced prisoners (10,500) and civil prisoners (200). There are about 7,200 sentenced young offenders under the age of 21 in custody. About 16 per cent of prisoners are from members of ethnic minorities as compared with 4.5 per cent in the population as a whole. In 1988, about 19 per cent of adult males sentenced to over 4 years were from ethnic minority groups as compared with under 9 per cent of those sentenced to up to 18 months. The population figures compare with a certified normal accommodation in the prisons of 45,400 on 30 June 1989. An intensive building programme is currently underway to provide additional accommodation to reduce overcrowding.

Figure 2

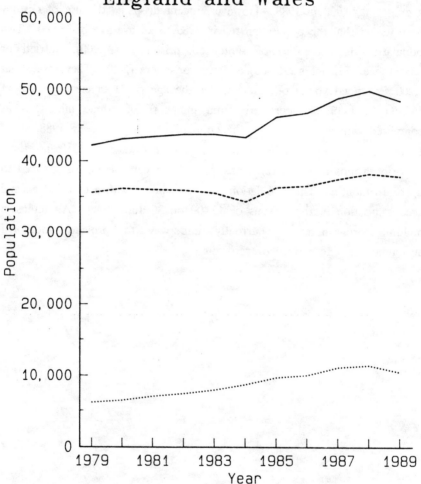

Average prison population
England and Wales

Total population Sentenced population

Remand population

8. FURTHER READING

8.1 Research and Statistics

The 1988 British Crime Survey, Pat Mayhew, David Elliot and Lizanne Dowds.

Criminal Statistics, England and Wales, 1988, HMSO

Judicial Statistics, 1988, HMSO

Prison Statistics, England and Wales, 1988, HMSO

General

The Sentence of the Court, Home Office, 1990.

Moriarty's Police Law (Numerous editions) London, Butterworth

Report of the Parole Board for 1988, HMSO

Report on the work of the Prison Service 1988/89, HMSO

Report of Her Majesty's Chief Inspector of Constabulary, 1988, HMSO

Report of Her Majesty's Chief Inspector of Prisons for England and Wales 1988, HMSO.

An Introduction to English Legal History, J. H. Baker, Butterworth

REFERENCES

(1)   Courts Act 1971

(2)   "A Criminal Code for England and Wales" (Law Commission No. 177 (HMSO 1989))

(3)   "The Criminal Law Review", p.141 (March 1990)

(4)   s.1 Police Act 1964

(5)   s.70 Justices of the Peace Act 1979

(6)   s.13-16 Justices of the Peace Act 1979

(7)   "Magistrates' Courts: Report of a Scrutiny", (HMSO 1989)

(8)   Children and Young Persons Act 1933

(9)   "Crime, Justice and Protecting the Public" (Cm 965)(HMSO 1990)

(10)   "Supervision and Punishment in the Community", (Home Office, 1990)

(11)   "Partnership in dealing with offenders in the Community"

(12)   "Report on the work of the Prison Service, April 1988-March 1989", (Cm 835)(HMSO 1989)

(13)   s.47 Prison Act 1952

(14)   Prison Rules 1964 - Statutory Instrument 388

(15)   Young Offender Institution - Statutory Instrument 1422

(16)   Prosecution of Offences Act 1985

(17)   s.50 Children and Young Persons Act 1933 as amended by s.16 Children and Young Persons Act 1963

(18)   s.1 Magistrates' Courts Act 1980

(19)   "Decision making in two English Police Forces", J B Morgan and D W B Webb (Exter 1984).

(20)   Schedule Part 1 Bail Act 1976

(21)   Criminal Law Act 1977

(22)   s.40 Criminal Justice Act 1988

(23)   s.12 Juries Act 1974 as amended by s.118 of the Criminal Justice Act 1988

(24)   Criminal Justice Act 1988

(25)   Murder (Abolition of Death Penalty) Act 1965

(26)   s.123 Criminal Justice Act 1988

(27)   s.1(4) Criminal Justice Act 1982

(28)   s.53 Children and Young Persons Act 1933

(29)   The Prison (Amendment) Rules 1987

(30)   "Victim's Charter: A Statement of the Rights of Victims of Crime" (HMSO,1990)

(31)   s.104 Criminal Justice Act 1988

(32)   The 1988 British Crime Survey, P. Mayhew, D. Elliot and L. Dowds, (HMSO, 1989)